Principles

PRINCIPLES OF MEDICAL ETHICS

PREFACE.

At the annual meeting of the American Medical Association, held in New Orleans, the House of Delegates unanimously adopted, on May 7, 1903, the "Principles of Medical Ethics" recommended by its committee, and ordered that the following extract from the report of the Special Committee on Revision of the Code of Medical Ethics be printed as an explanatory preface to these "Principles":

"The caption 'Principles of Medical Ethics' has been substituted for 'Code of Medical Ethics.' Inasmuch as the American Medical Association may be conceived to hold a relation to the constituent state associations analogous to that of the United States through its constitution to the several states, the committee deemed it wiser to formulate the principles of medical ethics without definite reference to code or penalties. Large discretionary powers are thus left to the respective state and territorial societies to form such codes and establish such rules for the professional conduct of their members as they may consider proper, provided, of course, that there shall be no infringement of the established ethical principles of this Association."

THE American Medical Association promulgates as a suggestive and advisory document the following:

CHAPTER I.

The Duties of Physicians to Their Patients.

―――――

THE PHYSICIAN'S RESPONSIBILITY.

SECTION 1.—Physicians should not only be ever ready to obey the calls of the sick and the injured, but should be mindful of the high character of their mission and of the responsibilities they must incur in the discharge of momentous duties. In their ministrations they should never forget that the comfort, the health and the lives of those entrusted to their care depend on skill, attention and fidelity. In deportment they should unite tenderness, cheerfulness and firmness, and thus inspire all sufferers with gratitude, respect and confidence. These observations are the more sacred because, generally, the only tribunal to adjudge penalties for unkindness, carelessness or neglect is their own conscience.

HUMANITY, DELICACY AND SECRECY NEEDED.

SEC. 2.—Every patient committed to the charge of a physician should be treated with attention and humanity, and reasonable indulgence should be granted to the caprices of the sick. Secrecy and delicacy should be strictly observed; and the familiar and confidential intercourse to which physicians are admitted, in their professional visits, should be guarded with the most scrupulous fidelity and honor.

SECRECY TO BE INVIOLATE.

SEC. 3.—The obligation of secrecy extends beyond the period of professional services; none of the privacies of individual or domestic life, no infirmity of disposition or flaw of character observed during medical attendance, should ever be divulged by physicians, except when imperatively required by the laws of the state. The force of the obligation of secrecy is so great that physicians have been protected in its observance by courts of justice.

FREQUENCY OF VISITS.

SEC. 4.—Frequent visits to the sick are often requisite, since they enable the physician to arrive at a more perfect knowledge of the disease, and to meet promptly every change which may occur. Unnecessary visits are to be *avoided, as they give undue anxiety to the patient; but to secure the patient against irritating suspense* and disappointment the regular *and periodical* visits of the physician should be made as nearly as possible at the hour when they may be reasonably expected by the patient.

HONESTY AND WISDOM IN PROGNOSIS.

SEC. 5.—Ordinarily, the physician should not be forward to make gloomy prognostications, but should not fail, on proper occasions, to give timely notice of dangerous manifestations to the friends of the patient; and even to the patient, if absolutely necessary. This notice, however, is at times so peculiarly alarming when given by the physician, that its deliverance may often be preferably assigned to another person of good judgment.

ENCOURAGEMENT OF PATIENTS.

SEC. 6.—The physician should be a minister of hope and comfort to the sick, since life may be lengthened or shortened not only by the acts, but by the words or manner of the physician, whose solemn duty is to avoid all utterances and actions having a tendency to discourage and depress the patient.

INCURABLE CASES NOT TO BE NEGLECTED.

SEC. 7.—The medical attendant ought not to *abandon* a patient because deemed incurable; *for continued* attention may be highly useful *to the* sufferer and comforting to the relative even in the last period of the fatal malady, by alleviating pain and by soothing mental anguish.

JUDICIOUS COUNSEL TO PATIENTS.

SEC. 8.—The opportunity which a physician has of promoting and strengthening the good resolutions of patients suffering under the consequences of evil conduct ought never to be neglected. Good counsels, or even remonstrances, will give satisfaction, not offense, if they be tactfully proffered and evince a genuine love of virtue, accompanied by a sincere interest in the welfare of the person to whom they are addressed.

CHAPTER II.

The Duties of Physicians to Each Other and to the Profession at Large.

ARTICLE I.—DUTIES FOR THE SUPPORT OF PROFESSIONAL CHARACTER.

OBLIGATION TO MAINTAIN THE HONOR OF THE PROFESSION.

SECTION 1.—Everyone on entering the profession, and thereby becoming entitled to full professional fellowship, incurs an obligation to uphold its dignity and honor, to exalt its standing and to extend the bounds of its usefulness. It is inconsistent with the principles of medical science and it is incompatible with honorable standing in the profession for physicians to designate their practice as based on an exclusive dogma or sectarian system of medicine.

OBSERVATION OF PROFESSIONAL RULES.

SEC. 2.—The physician should observe strictly such laws as are instituted for the government of the members of the profession; should honor the fraternity as a body; should endeavor to promote the science and art of medicine, and should entertain a due respect for those seniors who, by their labors, have contributed to its advancement.

DUTY TO JOIN MEDICAL ORGANIZATION.

SEC. 3.—Every physician should identify himself with the organized body of his profession as represented in the community in which he resides. The organization of local or county medical societies, where they do not exist, should be effected, so far as practicable. Such county societies, constituting as they do the chief element of strength in the organization of the profession, should have the active support of their members and should be made instruments for the cultivation of fellowship, for the exchange of professional experience, for the advancement of medical knowledge, for the maintenance of ethical standards, and for the promotion in general of the interests of the profession and the welfare of the public.

COUNTY SOCIETIES TO AFFILIATE WITH HIGHER ORGANIZATIONS.

SEC. 4.—All county medical societies thus *organized* ought to place themselves in affiliation *with* their respective state associations, *and these*, in turn, with the American Medical *Association.*

PURITY OF CHARACTER AND MORALITY REQUIRED.

SEC. 5.—There is no profession from the members of which greater purity of character and a higher standard of moral excellence are required than the medical; and to attain such eminence is a duty every physician owes alike to the profession and to patients. It is due to the patients, as without it their respect and confidence can not be commanded; and to the profession, because no scientific attainments can compensate for the want of correct moral principles.

TEMPERANCE IN ALL THINGS.

SEC. 6.—It is incumbent on physicians to be temperate in all things, for the practice of medicine requires the unremitting exercise of a clear and vigorous understanding; and in emergencies—for which no physician should be unprepared—a steady hand, an acute eye, and an unclouded mind are essential to the welfare and even to the life of a human being.

ADVERTISING METHODS TO BE AVOIDED.

SEC. 7.—It is incompatible with honorable standing in the profession to resort to public advertisement or private cards inviting the attention of persons affected with particular diseases; to promise radical cures; to publish cases or operations in the daily prints, or to suffer such publication to be made; to invite laymen ·(other than relatives who may desire to be at hand) to be present at operations; to boast of cures and remedies; to adduce certificates of skill and success, or to employ any of the other methods of charlatans.

PATENTS AND SECRET NOSTRUMS.

SEC. 8.—It is equally derogatory to professional character for physicians to hold patents for any surgical instruments or medicines; to accept rebates on prescriptions or surgical appliances; to assist unqualified persons to evade legal restrictions governing the practice of medicine; or to dispense, or promote the use of, secret medicines, for if such nostrums are of real efficacy, any concealment regarding them is inconsistent with beneficence and professional liberality, and if mystery alone give them public notoriety, such craft implies either disgraceful ignorance or fraudulent avarice. It is *highly* reprehensible for physicians to give *certificates* attesting the efficacy of secret medicines, or other substances used therapeutically.

ARTICLE II.—PROFESSIONAL SERVICES OF PHYSICIANS TO EACH OTHER.

PHYSICIANS DEPENDENT ON EACH OTHER.

SECTION 1.—Physicians should not, as a general rule, undertake the treatment of themselves, nor of members of their family. In such circumstances they are peculiarly dependent on each other; therefore, kind offices and professional aid should always .be cheerfully and gratuitously afforded. These visits ought not, however, to be obtrusively made, as they may give rise to embarrassment or interfere with that free choice on which such confidence depends.

GRATUITOUS SERVICES TO FELLOW PHYSICIANS.

SEC. 2.—All practicing physicians and their immediate family dependents are entitled to the gratuitous services of any one or more of the physicians residing near them.

COMPENSATION FOR EXPENSES.

SEC. 3.—When a physician is summoned from a distance to the bedside of a colleague in easy financial circumstances, a compensation, proportionate to traveling expenses and to the pecuniary loss entailed by absence from the accustomed field of professional labor, should be made by the patient or relatives.

ONE PHYSICIAN TO TAKE CHARGE.

SEC. 4.—When more than one physician is attending another, one of the number should take charge of the case, otherwise the concert of thought and action so essential to wise treatment can not be assured.

ATTENTION TO ABSENT PHYSICIAN'S PATIENTS.

SEC. 5.—The affairs of life, the pursuit of health, and the various accidents and contingencies to which a physician is peculiarly exposed, sometimes require the temporary withdrawal of this physician from daily professional labor and the appointment of a colleague to act for a specified time. The colleague's compliance is an act of courtesy which should always be performed with the utmost consideration for the interest and character of the family physician.

ARTICLE III.—THE DUTIES OF PHYSICIANS IN REGARD TO CONSULTATIONS.

THE BROADEST HUMANITY IN EMERGENCIES REQUIRED.

SECTION 1.—The broadest dictates of humanity should be obeyed by physicians whenever and wherever their services are needed to meet emergencies of disease or accident.

CONSULTATIONS SHOULD BE PROMOTED.

SEC. 2.—Consultations should be promoted in difficult cases, as they contribute to confidence and more enlarged views of practice.

PUNCTUALITY IN CONSULTATIONS.

SEC. 3.—The utmost punctuality should be observed in the visits of physicians when they are to hold consultations, and this is generally practicable, for society has been so considerate as to allow the plea for a professional engagement to take precedence over all others.

NECESSARY DELAYS.

SEC. 4.—As professional engagements may sometimes cause delay in attendance, the physician who first arrives should wait for a reasonable time, after which the consultation should be considered as postponed to a new appointment.

GOOD FEELING AND CANDOR IN CONSULTATIONS.

SEC. 5.—In consultations no insincerity, rivalry or envy should be indulged; candor, probity and all due respect should be observed toward the physician in charge of the case.

UNAUTHORIZED STATEMENTS OR DISCUSSIONS.

SEC. 6.—No statement or discussion of the case should take place before the patient or friends, except in the presence of all the physicians attending, or by their common consent; and no opinions or prognostications should be delivered which are not the result of previous deliberation and concurrence.

ATTENDING PHYSICIAN MAY VARY TREATMENT.

SEC. 7.—No decision should restrain the attending physician from making such subsequent variations in the mode of treatment as any unexpected change in the character of the case may demand. But at the next consultation reasons for the variations should be stated. The same privilege, with its obligation, belongs to the consultant when sent for in an emergency during the absence of the family physician.

ATTENDING PHYSICIAN TO PRESCRIBE.

SEC. 8.—The attending physician, at any time, may prescribe for the patient; not so the consultant, when alone, except in a case of emergency or when called from a considerable distance. In the first instance the consultant should do what is needed, and in the second should do no more than make an examination *of the patient* and leave a written opinion, *under seal,* to be delivered to the attending physician.

DISCUSSIONS IN CONSULTATION CONFIDENTIAL.

SEC. 9.—All discussions in consultation should be held as confidential. Neither by words nor by manner should any of the participants in a consultation assert or intimate that any part of the treatment pursued did not receive his assent.

CONFLICTS OF OPINION.

SEC. 10.—It may happen that two physicians can not agree in their views of the nature of a case and of the treatment to be pursued. In the event of such disagreement, a third physician should, if practicable, be called in. None but the rarest and most exceptional circumstances would justify the consultant in taking charge of the case. He should not do so merely on the solicitation of the patient or friends.

CONSULTANT TO SCRUPULOUSLY REGARD RIGHTS OF ATTENDING PHYSICIAN.

SEC. 11.—A physician who is called in consultation should observe the most honorable and scrupulous regard for the character and standing of the attending physician, whose conduct of the case should be justified, as far as can be, consistently with a conscientious regard for truth, and no hint or insinuation should be thrown out which would impair the confidence reposed in the attending physician.

ARTICLE IV.—DUTIES OF PHYSICIANS IN CASES OF INTERFERENCE.

QUALIFICATIONS THE ONLY BASIS OF PRACTICE.

SECTION 1.—Medicine being a liberal profession, those admitted to its ranks should found their expectations of practice especially on the character and extent of their medical education.

INTERCOURSE WITH PATIENTS OF OTHER PHYSICIANS.

SEC. 2.—The physician, in his intercourse with a patient under the care of another physician, should observe the strictest caution and reserve; should give no disingenuous hints relative to the nature and treatment of the patient's disorder, nor should the course of conduct of the physician, directly or indirectly, tend to diminish the trust reposed in the attending physician.

CIRCUMSPECTION AS REGARDS VISITS.

SEC. 3.—The same circumspection should be *observed* when, from motives of business or *friendship,* a physician is prompted to visit a *person* who is under the direction of another physician. Indeed, such visits should be avoided, except under peculiar circumstances; and when they are made, no inquiries should be instituted relative to the nature of the disease, or the remedies employed, but the topics of conversation should be as foreign to the case as circumstances will admit.

DUTY AS TO CALLS TO PATIENTS OF OTHER PHYSICIANS.

SEC. 4.—A physician ought not to take charge of, or prescribe for, a patient who has recently been under the care of another physician, in the same illness, except in case of a sudden emergency, or in consultation with the physician previously in attendance, or when that physician has relinquished the case or has been dismissed in due form.

CRITICISMS TO BE AVOIDED.

SEC. 5.—The physician acting in conformity with the preceding section should not make damaging insinuations regarding the practice adopted, and, indeed, should justify it if consistent with truth and probity; for it often happens that patients become dissatisfied when they are not immediately relieved, and, as many diseases are naturally protracted, th seeming want of success, in the first stage of treatment, affords no evidence of a lack of professional knowledge or skill.

EMERGENCY CASES.

SEC. 6.—When a physician is called to an urgent case, because the family attendant is not at hand, unless assistance in consultation is desired, the former should resign the care of the patient immediately on the arrival of the family physician.

DUTY WHEN CALLED WITH OTHER PHYSICIANS.

SEC. 7.—It often happens, in cases of sudden illness, and of accidents and injuries, owing to the alarm and anxiety of friends, that several physicians are simultaneously summoned. Under these circumstances, courtesy should assign the patient to the first who arrives, and who, if necessary, may invoke the aid of some of those present. In such case, however, the acting physician should request that the family physician be called, and should withdraw unless requested to continue in attendance.

CASE TO BE RELINQUISHED TO REGULAR ATTENDANT.

SEC. 8.—Whenever a physician is called to
˙·nt of another physician during the en-

forced absence of that physician the case should be relinquished on the return of the latter.

EMERGENCY ATTENTION AND ADVICE.

SEC. 9.—A physician, while visiting a sick person in the country, may be asked to see another physician's patient because of a sudden aggravation of the disease. On such an occasion the immediate needs of the patient should be attended to and the case relinquished on the arrival of the attending physician.

SUBSTITUTE OBSTETRIC WORK.

SEC. 10.—When a physician who has been engaged to attend an obstetric case is absent and another is sent for, delivery being accomplished during the vicarious attendance, the acting physician is entitled to the professional fee, but must resign the patient on the arrival of the physician first engaged.

ARTICLE V.—DIFFERENCES BETWEEN PHYSICIANS.

ARBITRATION OF DIFFERENCES.

SECTION 1.—Diversity of opinion and opposition of interest may, in the medical as in other professions, sometimes occasion controversy and even contention. Whenever such unfortunate cases occur and can not be immediately adjusted, they should be referred to the arbitration of a sufficient number of impartial physicians.

RESERVE TOWARD PUBLIC ON CERTAIN PROFESSIONAL QUESTIONS.

SEC. 2.—A peculiar reserve must be maintained by physicians toward the public in regard to some professional questions, and as there exist many points in medical ethics and etiquette through which the feelings of physicians may be painfully assailed in their intercourse, and which can not be understood or appreciated by general society, neither the subject-matter of their differences nor the adjudication of the arbitration should be made public.

ARTICLE VI.—COMPENSATION.

THE LIMITS OF GRATUITOUS SERVICE.

SECTION 1.—By the members of no profession are eleemosynary services more liberally dispensed than by the medical, but justice requires that some limits should be placed to their performance. Poverty, mutual professional obligations, and certain of the public *duties* named in Sections 1 and 2 of Chapter *III, should always* be recognized as presenting valid claims for gratuitous services; but neither institutions endowed by the public or the rich, or by societies for mutual benefit, for life insurance, or for analogous purposes, nor any profession or occupation, can be admitted to possess such privilege.

CERTIFYING OR TESTIFYING TO BE PAID FOR.

SEC. 2.—It can not be justly expected of physicians to furnish certificates of inability to serve on juries, or to perform militia duty; to testify to the state of health of persons wishing to insure their lives, obtain pensions, or the like, without due compensation. But to persons in indigent circumstances such services should always be cheerfully and freely accorded.

FEE BILLS.

SEC. 3.—Some general rules should be adopted by the physicians in every town or district relative to the minimum pecuniary acknowledgement from their patients; and it should be deemed a point of honor to adhere to these rules with as much uniformity as varying circumstances will admit.

GIVING OR RECEIVING OF COMMISSIONS CONDEMNED.

SEC. 4.—It is derogatory to professional character for physicians to pay or offer to no commissions to any person whatsoever who may recommend to them patients requiring general or special treatment or surgical operations. It is equally derogatory to professional character for physicians to solicit or to receive such commissions.

CHAPTER III.

The Duties of the Profession to the Public.

DUTIES AS TO PUBLIC HYGIENE, ETC.

SECTION 1.—As good citizens it is the duty of physicians to be very vigilant for the welfare of the community, and to bear their part in sustaining its laws, institutions and burdens; especially should they be ready to coöperate with the proper authorities in the administration and the observance of sanitary laws and regulations, and they should also be ever ready to give counsel to the public in relation to subjects especially appertaining to their profession, as on questions of sanitary police, public hygiene and legal medicine.

ENLIGHTENMENT OF PUBLIC ON SANITARY MATTERS.—DUTIES IN EPIDEMICS.

SEC. 2.—It is the province of physicians to enlighten the public in regard to quarantine regulations; to the location, arrangement and dietaries of hospitals, asylums, schools, prisons and similar institutions; in regard to measures for the prevention of epidemic and contagious diseases; and when pestilence prevails, it is their duty to face the danger, and to continue their labors for the alleviation of the suffering people, even at the risk of their own lives.

PHYSICIANS AS WITNESSES.

SEC. 3.—Physicians, when called on by legally constituted authorities, should always be ready to enlighten inquests and courts of justice on subjects strictly medical, such as involve questions relating to sanity, legitimacy, murder by poison or other violent means, and various other subjects embraced in the science of medical jurisprudence. It is but just, however, for them to expect due compensation for their services.

ENLIGHTENMENT OF THE PUBLIC AS TO CHARLATANS.

SEC. 4.—It is the duty of physicians who are frequent witnesses of the great wrongs committed by charlatans and of the injury to health and even destruction of life caused by the use of their treatment, to enlighten the public on these subjects and to make known the injuries sustained by the unwary from the devices and pretensions of artful impostors.

RELATIONS TO PHARMACISTS.

SEC. 5.—It is the duty of physicians to recognize and by legitimate patronage to promote the profession of pharmacy, on the skill and proficiency of which depends the reliability of remedies, but any pharmacist who, although educated in his own profession, is not a qualified physician, and who assumes to prescribe for the sick, ought not to receive such countenance and support. Any druggist or pharmacist who dispenses deteriorated or sophisticated drugs or who substitutes one remedy for another designated in a prescription ought thereby to forfeit the recognition and influence of physicians.

INDEX TO PRINCIPLES OF ETHICS